G. ALLEN JACKSON

S0-ASU-639

TODAY...
I WILL

---

30 DAYS OF PRAYER

Intend
PUBLISHING

© 2015 by G. Allen Jackson
ISBN 978-1-61718-035-4

Published by Intend Publishing
Murfreesboro, Tennessee

Cover Design by Kim Russell / Wahoo Designs
Page Layout by Bart Dawson

Printed in the United States of America

1 2 3 4 5—CHG—19 18 17 16 15

TABLE OF CONTENTS

INTRODUCTION

Welcome to thirty days of hope and possibility. Prayer changes things. People who pray make a difference. Take the prayers in this book and make them yours. Offer them to God. You can pray them for yourself, with a friend, or as a family. The purposes of God emerge as His people pray.

As you begin to let prayer have a new place in your life, begin to listen in new ways as well. God's thoughts will arrive in your life—through the words of a friend, the lyric of a song, a passage of Scripture, a still small voice. Prayer is the amazing privilege of a relationship with Almighty God. The goal of prayer is not the recruitment of God to do our bidding but a transformation within us that allows God's purposes to move forward.

CHAPTER 1

TODAY, I WILL SERVE THE LORD

PRAYER FOR THE DAY

Come Holy Spirit, You are welcome in my life. Give me eyes to see and ears to hear—I choose to cooperate with You. Grant me a revelation of the Living God. Help me to honor Jesus of Nazareth in my life. Bring understanding of God's provision for my life—His love, His great power expressed towards me and through me. May the hope of the Living God surround my life today. In Jesus' name, amen.

EPHESIANS 1:17

I keep asking that the God of our Lord Jesus Christ, the glorious Father, may give you the Spirit of wisdom and revelation, so that you may know him better.

TODAY'S THOUGHTS ABOUT SERVING GOD

A servant of God has but one Master.

George Mueller

In Jesus the service of God and the service of the
least of the bretheren were one.

Dietrich Bonhoeffer

We serve God by serving people.

Allen Jackson

What is needed for happy effectual service is simply
to put your work into the Lord's hand,
and leave it there.

Hannah Whitall Smith

Timely service, like timely gifts, is doubled in value.

George MacDonald

When you truly know God,
you have energy to serve him,
boldness to share him, and contentment in him.

J. I. Packer

Faithful servants never retire.
You can retire from your career,
but you will never retire from serving God.

Rick Warren

A true servant of God is one who helps
another succeed.

Billy Graham

Have thy tools ready;
God will find thee work.

Charles Kingsley

Date: *April 2, 2021*

Give Thanks: today I am thankful for . . .

My car fixed

My Plumbing Fixed

That God supplied the money

My children + grandchildren

my Brother + Peggy

Worry Free: today I will lay aside all anxiety regarding . . .

My mis-placed Box of diamond Jewelry - Oh Lord I place them in your hands and Thank you that they are found soon

Serving God: today I will serve the Lord through . . .

Tithing

Paying my Bills -

Wherever He leads

CHAPTER 2

TODAY, I WILL REJOICE

PRAYER FOR THE DAY

Heavenly Father, I rejoice today in Your majesty and power. In You, I have hope and a future. Thank You for Your abundant provision and careful protection of our lives. Today, I choose humility and acknowledge You as my Creator and Redeemer. I gratefully serve You as Lord. Lord Jesus, may I bring glory and honor to Your name. Amen.

COLOSSIANS 3:17

And whatever you do, whether in word or deed, do it all in the name of the Lord Jesus, giving thanks to God the Father through him.

TODAY'S THOUGHTS ABOUT JOY

Thankfulness will dispel anxiety in your life.
Start your day by telling God "Thank You."

Allen Jackson

Joy comes not from what we have
but what we are.

C. H. Spurgeon

This is the happy life, to rejoice to Thee, of Thee,
for Thee; this it is, and there is no other.

St. Augustine

Happy is the person who has learned to rejoice in
the simple and beautiful things around him.

Billy Graham

Joy is the simplest form of gratitude.

Karl Barth

The world looks for happiness through
self-assertion. The Christian knows that joy is
found in self-abandonment.

Elisabeth Elliot

What think we of Christ? Is He altogether glorious
in our eyes, and precious to our hearts?
May Christ be our joy, our confidence, our all.

Matthew Henry

Joy is the great note all throughout the Bible.

Oswald Chambers

Joy is the serious business of heaven.

C. S. Lewis

Date: April 6, 2021

Give Thanks: today I am thankful for . . .

You saved me God,
You forgave my sins
You gave me eternal life
You provide for me
You give me wisdom
you give me health

Worry Free: today I will lay aside all anxiety regarding . . .

my mis-placed diamonds
my inability to travel
my regrets of the past

Serving God: today I will serve the Lord through . . .

Reading devotionals —
Meeting my neighbor
Listening for His voice
and being obedient to
what He tells me —
Help me to listen carefully
to you Oh, Lord —

CHAPTER 3

TODAY, I WILL TRUST GOD'S PROVISION

PRAYER FOR THE DAY

I know You are my deliverer. I rejoice today in Your provision and protection for my life. Forgive my ingratitude and stubbornness. I choose to yield to You, to follow Your direction, and to obey Your instruction. I choose to believe; help my unbelief. May Your Word become a living reality within me. In Jesus' name, amen.

PSALM 18:2

The LORD is my rock, my fortress and my deliverer; my God is my rock, in whom I take refuge. He is my shield and the horn of my salvation, my stronghold.

TODAY'S THOUGHTS ABOUT GOD'S PROVISION

God is trying to get a message through to you, and
the message is: "Stop depending on inadequate
human resources. Let me handle the matter."

Catherine Marshall

The center of God's will is our only safety.

Betsie ten Boom

No situation is beyond God's control.
Over my wife's desk are these words:
"Fear not for the future. God is already there."

Billy Graham

A mighty fortress is our God, a bulwark
never failing, our helper he amid
the flood of mortal ills prevailing.

Martin Luther

God alone can give us songs in the night.

C. H. Spurgeon

No difficulties can baffle Him if you will only put yourselves absolutely into His hands and let Him have His own way with you.

Hannah Whitall Smith

God is sufficient for all our needs, for every problem, for every difficulty, for every broken heart, for every human sorrow.

Peter Marshall

The knowledge that we are never alone calms the troubled sea of our lives and speaks peace to our souls.

A. W. Tozer

Date: _04/07/2021_

Give Thanks: today I am thankful for . . .

God setting me free from torment
over my mother's death —
Thank you Jesus

Worry Free: today I will lay aside all anxiety
regarding . . .

my past.

Serving God: today I will serve the Lord through . . .

prayer & Thanksgiving —
and finding a Bible for
Noah and Emma —
Lord help me to choose
the right ones!

CHAPTER 4

TODAY, I WILL SEEK GOD'S GUIDANCE

PRAYER FOR THE DAY

Heavenly Father, as we gather today may a spirit of worship and reverence fill our hearts. We choose to consecrate ourselves for Your purposes in our lives. Our desire is to walk in the light of God's truth, in the strength of fellowship with one another, and under the guidance of Your Spirit. Thank You for Your leading and careful protection of our lives. In Jesus' name, amen.

1 JOHN 1:7

But if we walk in the light, as he is in the light, we have fellowship with one another, and the blood of Jesus, his Son, purifies us from all sin.

TODAY'S THOUGHTS ABOUT GOD'S GUIDANCE

I am satisfied that when the Almighty wants me
to do or not to do any particular thing,
he finds a way to let me know it.

Abraham Lincoln

A possibility is a hint from God.

Søren Kierkegaard

Time spent in prayer will yield more than that
given to work. Prayer alone gives work its worth
and its success. Prayer opens the way for God
Himself to do His work in us and through us.

Andrew Murray

God will never—never—lead you to do something
that is contrary to his written Word, the Bible.

Billy Graham

Often God has to shut a door in our face
so that he can subsequently open the door
through which he wants us to go.

Catherine Marshall

When we are obedient, God guides
our steps and our stops.

Corrie ten Boom

We have ample evidence that the Lord is able
to guide. The promises cover every imaginable
situation. All we need to do is to take
the hand he stretches out.

Elisabeth Elliot

We have to live as if eternity matters.

Allen Jackson

Date: _04-08-2021_

Give Thanks: today I am thankful for . . .

God! Ron & Laura Wade
Martha Conner - Nelda -
Elsie - David - Janet -
Cynthia - Sat Sisters

Worry Free: today I will lay aside all anxiety regarding . . .

My assignment - What
God has called me to do
He will equip me

Serving God: today I will serve the Lord through . . .

Taking Elsie to eat
Mailing letter to Editor
Giving Ron $1000 for His Book

CHAPTER 5

TODAY, I WILL SEEK GOD'S PEACE

PRAYER FOR THE DAY

Heavenly Father, my life is open before You; I desire to hide nothing. May Your grace and mercy surround me, Your peace fill my heart, and Your Spirit sustain my body. Let Your dreams fill my life. May Your word take root within me. Open my eyes to see Your purposes. I rejoice in the privilege of serving You, my Lord and my Redeemer. Amen.

PHILIPPIANS 4:7

And the peace of God, which transcends all understanding, will guard your hearts and your minds in Christ Jesus.

TODAY'S THOUGHTS ABOUT GOD'S PEACE

Peace and freedom from fear are linked to our
cooperation with the person of the Holy Spirit.

Allen Jackson

The knowledge that we are never alone calms
the troubled sea of our lives and speaks
peace to our souls.

A. W. Tozer

When our lives are filled with peace, faith and joy,
people will want to know what we have.

David Jeremiah

The Christian needs to walk in peace, so no matter
what happens they will be able to bear witness
to a watching world.

Henry Blackaby

God, you have made us for yourself, and our hearts
are restless till they find their rest in you.

St. Augustine

What peace can they have who are not
at peace with God?

Matthew Henry

Emotional peace and calm come after doing
God's will and not before.

Erwin Lutzer

God, give us the grace to accept with serenity
the things that cannot be changed, the courage to
change the things that should be changed, and
the wisdom to distinguish the one from the other.

Reinhold Niebuhr

Thank Friday G. Allen Jackson

Date: April 09 - 2021

Give Thanks: today I am thankful for . . .

Laura Wade — she listened
while I cried about the rape
in OKC — She prayed and
I was set free — able to
forgive myself —

Worry Free: today I will lay aside all anxiety

regarding . . .

My past — Jesus paid
the price so I could be
a Victor — Not a Victum

Serving God: today I will serve the Lord through . . .

Helping others —
Sending cards —
Being led by the Spirit
Taking Nelda to get donuts

CHAPTER 6

TODAY, I WILL FOCUS ON JESUS

PRAYER FOR THE DAY

Heavenly Father, I rejoice in my place in Your kingdom; by Your great mercy and power, You have made me welcome through faith in Jesus. I know that my Redeemer lives. My hope is anchored by the sacrifice of my High Priest. I rejoice that every obstacle, need, or challenge must yield before the majesty of the King of kings and Lord of lords. Through faith in Jesus, my life is a testimony of His great victory, amen.

HEBREWS 12:2

Let us fix our eyes on Jesus, the author and perfecter of our faith . . .

TODAY'S THOUGHTS ABOUT FOCUSING ON JESUS

The central message of the Bible is Jesus Christ.

Billy Graham

Christ is either Lord of all, or He is not Lord at all.

Hudson Taylor

Jesus is not coming back to the earth to recruit a new team—He's coming back to the earth for the people who have put their faith in Him and believed in Him.

Allen Jackson

Never try to arouse faith from within. You cannot stir up faith from the depths of your heart. Leave your heart, and look into the face of Christ.

Andrew Murray

The beautiful thing about this adventure called
faith is that we can count on Him
never to lead us astray.

Charles Swindoll

Be assured, if you walk with Him and look to Him,
and expect help from Him, He will never fail you.

George Mueller

If Jesus is the Son of God, his teachings
are more than just good ideas from a wise teacher;
they are divine insights on which
I can confidently build my life.

Lee Strobel

Jesus gives us hope because He keeps us company,
has a vision and knows the way we should go.

Max Lucado

Date: 04-00-2021

Give Thanks: today I am thankful for . . .

deliverance - for at
long last being on -in-
good soil (Jesus Christ)

Worry Free: today I will lay aside all anxiety
regarding . . .

FAiled

The things I have ~~failed~~
in - not accomplished

Serving God: today I will serve the Lord through . . .

~~Obtaining needed~~ Welcoming
Jan + Kris Krebs -
Try to make their
visit good

CHAPTER 7

TODAY, I WILL BE THANKFUL

PRAYER FOR THE DAY

Heavenly Father, open my heart and soul to what Jesus has done for me. Holy Spirit, grant me a revelation of my Lord and Redeemer. I believe that through Jesus' sacrifice I have been redeemed out of an empty way of life, delivered from satanic bondage, and welcomed into the eternal kingdom of God. I rejoice today in my Lord and the great liberty He has brought to my life. In Jesus' name, amen.

PSALM 19:14

May the words of my mouth and the meditation of my heart be pleasing in your sight, O LORD, my Rock and my Redeemer.

TODAY'S THOUGHTS ABOUT GRATITUDE

The pathway to the presence of God is marked out
for us with praise and thanksgiving.

Allen Jackson

Gratitude is one of the greatest Christian virtues;
ingratitude, one of the most vicious sins.

Billy Graham

It is only with gratitude that life becomes rich.

Dietrich Bonhoeffer

To be grateful is to recognize the love of God
in everything He has given us—
and He has given us everything.

Thomas Merton

Thanksgiving will draw our hearts out to God
and keep us engaged with Him.

Andrew Murray

A true Christian is a person who never for
a moment forgets what God has done.
He is a man whose comportment and activities
have their root in the sentiment of gratitude.

John Baillie

No matter what our circumstance,
we can find a reason to be thankful.

David Jeremiah

Worries flee before a spirit of gratitude.

Billy Graham

G. Allen Jackson

Sunday

Date: 04/11/2021

Give Thanks: today I am thankful for . . .

Jane & Kris Krebs

Worry Free: today I will lay aside all anxiety regarding . . .

money - he who lendeth or giveth to the poor God will Repay

Serving God: today I will serve the Lord through . . .

Serving Kris & Jan -
Giving them Breakfast
Helping find Phone # $
$ 50 cash to each -

Monday

CHAPTER 8

TODAY, I WILL HUMBLE MYSELF BEFORE GOD

PRAYER FOR THE DAY

Thank You for Your great provision for my life. I rejoice in the fullness of my salvation. My desire is to honor You with my entire being. May Your Spirit open my eyes to any place within me that limits Your purposes. I choose life. I choose obedience. I choose to humble myself. I choose Jesus as my Lord. I choose to complete the course designed for me. Grant me the strength and courage to align my will with Your invitations. In Jesus' name, amen.

PROVERBS 22:4

Humility and the fear of the LORD bring wealth and honor and life.

TODAY'S THOUGHTS ABOUT HUMILITY

Modesty is the badge of wisdom.

Matthew Henry

Yielding to the wisdom and direction and the insight of Almighty God is a good pattern to build into your life.

Allen Jackson

Christ is the humility of God embodied in human nature; the Eternal Love humbling itself, clothing itself in the garb of meekness and gentleness, to win and serve and save us.

Andrew Murray

Pride builds walls between people, humility builds bridges.

Rick Warren

Do you wish to be great? Think first about the
foundations of humility. The higher your structure
is to be, the deeper must be its foundation.

St. Augustine

The one true way of dying to self is
the way of patience, meekness, humility,
and resignation to God.

Andrew Murray

Not until we have become humble and teachable,
standing in awe of God's holiness and sovereignty,
distrusting our own thoughts, and willing
to have our minds turned upside down,
can divine wisdom become ours.

J. I. Packer

A person wrapped up in himself
makes a small package.

Harry Emerson Fosdick

Monday

Date: _April 12th - 2021_

Give Thanks: today I am thankful for . . .

Doctors?

Friends

Worry Free: today I will lay aside all anxiety regarding . . .

Doctors

Serving God: today I will serve the Lord through . . .

Spending time with Him -

Praising + Thanking Him

CHAPTER 9

TODAY, I WILL SEEK GOD'S PURPOSE

PRAYER FOR THE DAY

I rejoice in Your great mercy and grace. May my heart be open to You; enable me to recognize Your pathway and grant me the courage to choose Your best. May my life be a strength to Your people and enable Your purposes to be accomplished more fully in the earth. Thank You for loving me, accepting me, and bringing purpose to my life. In Jesus' name, amen.

EPHESIANS 2:10

For we are God's workmanship, created in Christ Jesus to do good works, which God prepared in advance for us to do.

TODAY'S THOUGHTS ABOUT
SEEKING GOD'S PURPOSE

The easiest way to discover the purpose of
an invention is to ask the creator of it.
The same is true for discovering
your life's purpose: Ask God.

Rick Warren

What is my life purpose O'God?

You aren't an accident. You were deliberately
planned, specifically gifted, and lovingly
positioned on this earth by the Master Craftsman.

Max Lucado

What is my "Special Gift"?

Our purpose should be to discover the gifts
He has given us and to use those gifts faithfully
and joyfully in His service, without either envying
or disparaging the gifts we do not have.

John MacArthur

Don't waste your life on things that
have no eternal value.

Billy Graham

God is the silent partner in all great enterprises.

Abraham Lincoln

Underneath each trouble there is
a faithful purpose.

C. H. Spurgeon

The cross gives a new purpose to life.

Billy Graham

There is nothing quite as potent as a focused life,
one lived on purpose.

Rick Warren

Date: _April 15th 2021_

Give Thanks: today I am thankful for . . .

The decision I made about
Dr. Lewis — Thankful for
the VA and for Wellness Clinic —
Thankful for God's mercy
+ Loving Kindness

Worry Free: today I will lay aside all anxiety
regarding . . .

my health —

May I rest well
feel better soon

Serving God: today I will serve the Lord through . . .

Being Obedient
Loving Him
Rejoicing that I am alive!

CHAPTER 10

TODAY, I WILL SEEK GOD'S PATH

PRAYER FOR THE DAY

Heavenly Father, I acknowledge You as the source of my life. Thank You for Your extravagant provision on my behalf. I choose to walk in Your path; may Your abiding presence bring distinction to my life. I repent of all compromise and rebellious attitudes. I want to cooperate fully with You. May Your people humble themselves before You and seek Your face that healing may come to our land. In Jesus' name, amen.

ISAIAH 1:18-19

"Come now, let us reason together," says the LORD. "Though your sins are like scarlet, they shall be as white as snow; though they are red as crimson, they shall be like wool. If you are willing and obedient, you will eat the best from the land."

TODAY'S THOUGHTS ABOUT SEEKING GOD'S PATH

The best things are nearest: breath in your nostrils,
light in your eyes, flowers at your feet, duties
at your hand, the path of God before you.

Robert Louis Stevenson

If not a sparrow falls upon the ground without
your Father; you have reason to see the smallest
events of your career are arranged by him.

C. H. Spurgeon

Life is about letting God use you for his purposes,
not using him for your own purpose.

Rick Warren

I find that doing of the will of God leaves me
no time for disputing about His plans.

George MacDonald

A saint's life is in the hands of God as a bow and
arrow in the hands of an archer. God is aiming at
something the saint cannot see.

Oswald Chambers

When God is involved, anything can happen.
Be open. Stay that way. God has a beautiful way of
bringing good vibrations out of broken chords.

Charles Swindoll

God does not give us everything we want,
but He does fulfill His promises, leading us along
the best and straightest paths to Himself.

Dietrich Bonhoeffer

If all things are possible with God, then all things
are possible to him who believes in Him.

Corrie ten Boom

Date:_____

Give Thanks: today I am thankful for . . .

_____

_____

_____

_____

_____

Worry Free: today I will lay aside all anxiety
regarding . . .

_____

_____

_____

_____

Serving God: today I will serve the Lord through . . .

_____

_____

_____

_____

_____

_____

CHAPTER 11

TODAY, I WILL TRUST GOD'S WORD

PRAYER FOR THE DAY

Heavenly Father, thank You for the privilege of hearing Your Word. I choose to open my heart and receive all You have for me. I say yes to You; I want to be cooperative. Forgive my sins, my rebellion, and my idolatry. Apart from You I have no hope. In You there is mercy and forgiveness. I rejoice in Your faithfulness. May my life be pleasing in Your sight. Amen.

HEBREWS 4:12

For the word of God is living and active. Sharper than any double-edged sword, it penetrates even to dividing soul and spirit, joints and marrow; it judges the thoughts and attitudes of the heart.

G. Allen Jackson

TODAY'S THOUGHTS ABOUT
GOD'S WORD

Give time to reading the Bible, and the renewing
effect is as real as that of breathing fresh air.

Oswald Chambers

A new world will arise when we approach
our Bible with the idea that it is a book
that is now speaking.

A. W. Tozer

Each of us has a reference point. As a Christian,
the reference point by which I measure my life
and my thought is the Bible.

Billy Graham

Nobody ever outgrows the scriptures;
the book widens and deepens with our years.

C. H. Spurgeon

The vigor of our spiritual life will be in exact
proportion to the place held by the Bible
in our life and thoughts.

George Mueller

The Bible grows more beautiful as we grow
in our understanding of it.

Goethe

God's Book is packed with overwhelming riches.
They are unsearchable—the more we have,
the more there is to have.

Oswald Chambers

God uses his Word, people and circumstances
to mold us. All three are indispensable
for character development.

Rick Warren

Date:_____

Give Thanks: today I am thankful for . . .

_____

_____

_____

_____

_____

Worry Free: today I will lay aside all anxiety regarding . . .

_____

_____

_____

_____

Serving God: today I will serve the Lord through . . .

_____

_____

_____

_____

_____

_____

CHAPTER 12

TODAY, I WILL REJOICE IN THE GIFT OF SALVATION

PRAYER FOR THE DAY

Heavenly Father, I rejoice today in my salvation. Open the eyes of my understanding to the great gift of Jesus. Help me to recognize Your great strength and power exerted on my behalf. May my life bring glory to Your Son. May the words of my mouth exalt Jesus each day. Allow my years to become an offering of thanksgiving to my Lord, Jesus Christ. In His name, we lift our voices this day, amen.

PSALM 7:17

I will give thanks to the Lord because of his righteousness and will sing praise to the name of the Lord Most High.

TODAY'S THOUGHTS ABOUT
THE GIFT OF SALVATION

Salvation comes through a cross
and a crucified Christ.

Andrew Murray

God doesn't say you have to be perfect to get to
heaven. He says you have to come to the cross,
and whosoever shall call upon the name
of the Lord shall be saved.

Billy Graham

Your actions of being nice will not get you into
Heaven. You have to believe.

Allen Jackson

Jesus became mortal to give you immortality;
and today, through Him, you can be free.

David Jeremiah

God is not saving the world; it is done.
Our business is to get men and women to realize it.

Oswald Chambers

At most, you will live a hundred years on earth,
but you will spend forever in eternity.

Rick Warren

Salvation is by Christ alone, through faith alone,
for the glory of God alone.

Billy Graham

There is no one so far lost that Jesus cannot find
him and cannot save him.

Andrew Murray

Date:_____

Give Thanks: today I am thankful for . . .

_____

_____

_____

_____

_____

Worry Free: today I will lay aside all anxiety
regarding . . .

_____

_____

_____

_____

Serving God: today I will serve the Lord through . . .

_____

_____

_____

_____

_____

_____

CHAPTER 13

TODAY, I WILL GIVE THANKS FOR GOD'S PROTECTION

PRAYER FOR THE DAY

Heavenly Father, thank You for reaching out to me. You came to me when I was desperate and alone and extended grace and mercy to me. You have made provision for my sin, provided guidance for my life, demonstrated patience when I have been rebellious, and protected me when I was unable to defend myself. Your great love has lifted my life from a place of despair to a pathway of opportunity. I rejoice in Your Word, I want to cooperate with Your Spirit, and I desire to live for the glory of Your Son. May my life be a living testimony of Your majesty and glory. Amen.

PSALM 116:8-9

For you, O LORD, have delivered my soul from death, my eyes from tears, my feet from stumbling, that I may walk before the LORD in the land of the living.

TODAY'S THOUGHTS ABOUT GOD'S PROTECTION

The safest place in all the world is in the will
of God, and the safest protection in all
the world is the name of God.

Warren Wiersbe

Seek your security in anything but God
and you will never find it.

St. Stephen of Muret

With the goodness of God to desire our highest
welfare, the wisdom of God to plan it, and the
power of God to achieve it, what do we lack?
The answer, of course, is that we lack nothing.

A. W. Tozer

Discipline yourself to stay close to God.
He alone is your security.

Billy Graham

I refuse to become panicky, as I lift up my eyes to
Him and accept it as coming from the throne
of God for some great purpose of blessing
to my own heart.

Alan Redpath

As you walk through the valley of the unknown,
you will find the footprints of Jesus both
in front of you and beside you.

Charles Stanley

Where does your security lie? Is God your refuge,
your hiding place, your stronghold, your shepherd,
your counselor, your friend, your redeemer, your
savior, your guide? If He is, you don't need to
search any further for security.

Elisabeth Elliot

The center of God's will is our only safety.

Corrie ten Boom

Date:_____

Give Thanks: today I am thankful for . . .

_____

_____

_____

_____

_____

Worry Free: today I will lay aside all anxiety
regarding . . .

_____

_____

_____

_____

Serving God: today I will serve the Lord through . . .

_____

_____

_____

_____

_____

_____

CHAPTER 14

TODAY, I WILL CHOOSE TO BE OBEDIENT

PRAYER FOR THE DAY

Heavenly Father, today I choose obedience—to turn my heart toward You afresh. May Your Spirit bring awareness of anything that impedes my progress with You. I desire to fulfill my created purpose. Grant me the strength and courage to embrace the truth and overcome all obstacles. Stretch out Your hand to deliver, heal, and restore. My trust is in You, my Lord and my Redeemer. May the power of the Living God be made evident in my life. In Jesus' name, amen.

PROVERBS 1:33

But whoever listens to me will live in safety and be at ease, without fear of harm.

TODAY'S THOUGHTS ABOUT OBEDIENCE

We glorify God by living lives that honor Him.

Billy Graham

When we are obedient,
God guides our steps and our stops.

Corrie ten Boom

Faith and obedience are inescapably related.

John MacArthur

God has laid down spiritual laws which, if obeyed,
bring harmony and fulfillment, but, if disobeyed,
bring discord and disorder.

Billy Graham

The golden rule for understanding in spiritual
matters is not intellect, but obedience.

Oswald Chambers

You can only learn what obedience is by obeying.

Dietrich Bonhoeffer

You cannot obey God without your obedience
spilling out in a blessing to all those around you.

Adrian Rogers

Cultivate prompt, exact, unquestioning, joyous
obedience to every command that it is evident from
its context applies to you. Be on the lookout for
new orders from your King. Blessing lies in
the direction of obedience to them.

R. A. Torrey

Date:_____

Give Thanks: today I am thankful for . . .

_____

_____

_____

_____

_____

Worry Free: today I will lay aside all anxiety regarding . . .

_____

_____

_____

_____

Serving God: today I will serve the Lord through . . .

_____

_____

_____

_____

_____

_____

CHAPTER 15

TODAY, I WILL BE BOLD IN MY FAITH

PRAYER FOR THE DAY

I choose to believe, to lead a life of faith in Jesus Christ. May the Spirit of the Living God grant me a revelation of Jesus that unleashes new steps of faith, brings great boldness, and enables my life to honor my Lord as never before. In Jesus' name, amen.

JOHN 20:31

But these are written that you may believe that Jesus is the Christ, the Son of God, and that by believing you may have life in his name.

TODAY'S THOUGHTS ABOUT FAITH

Faith expects from God what is beyond
all expectation.

Andrew Murray

Faith points us beyond our problems
to the hope we have in Christ.

Billy Graham

Faith and obedience are bound up in the same
bundle. He that obeys God, trusts God;
and he that trusts God, obeys God.

C. H. Spurgeon

Meet your fears with faith.

Max Lucado

Faith is the assurance that the thing which
God has said in His word is true,
and that God will act according to
what He has said.

George Mueller

Faith is an activity.
It is something that has to be applied.

Corrie ten Boom

Our praying, to be strong,
must be buttressed by holy living.
The life of faith perfects the prayer of faith.

E. M. Bounds

Faith is born at the Cross of Christ.

C. H. Spurgeon

Date:_____

Give Thanks: today I am thankful for . . .

_____

_____

_____

_____

_____

Worry Free: today I will lay aside all anxiety
regarding . . .

_____

_____

_____

_____

Serving God: today I will serve the Lord through . . .

_____

_____

_____

_____

_____

_____

CHAPTER 16

TODAY, I WILL BE ENTHUSIASTIC, NOT INDIFFERENT

PRAYER FOR THE DAY

Heavenly Father, thank You for the Body of Christ. Forgive me for being critical of Your people. I repent of indifference and distraction. May the purposes of the Living God be ignited within my heart. Enable me to use my life to serve You and Your people. May Your Church awaken to the opportunities of this generation and boldly proclaim the Lordship of Jesus of Nazareth. In Jesus' name, amen.

ACTS 4:29-30

Now, Lord, consider their threats and enable your servants to speak your word with great boldness. Stretch out your hand to heal and perform miraculous signs and wonders through the name of your holy servant Jesus.

TODAY'S THOUGHTS ABOUT ENTHUSIASM

We act as though comfort and luxury were the chief requirements of life, when all that we need to make us really happy is something to be enthusiastic about.

Charles Kingsley

When you sense an invitation from God—cooperate!

Allen Jackson

Wherever you are, be all there. Live to the hilt every situation you believe to be the will of God.

Jim Elliot

Those who have achieved excellence in the practice of an art or profession have commonly been motivated by great enthusiasm in their pursuit of it.

John Knox

Positive thinking is how you think about
a problem. Enthusiasm is how you feel about
a problem. The two together determine what
you do about a problem.

Norman Vincent Peale

Consider each day, as it were, a beginning,
and always act with the same fervour as
on the first day you began.

St. Anthony of Padua

Leave not off reading the Bible till you find
your hearts warmed.
Let it not only inform you but inflame you.

Thomas Watson

Good words are worth much and cost little.

George Herbert

Date:_____

Give Thanks: today I am thankful for . . .

_____

_____

_____

_____

_____

Worry Free: today I will lay aside all anxiety
regarding . . .

_____

_____

_____

_____

Serving God: today I will serve the Lord through . . .

_____

_____

_____

_____

_____

_____

CHAPTER 17

TODAY, I WILL BE HOPEFUL

PRAYER FOR THE DAY

Heavenly Father, thank You for making a new life possible for me. In Christ I have been delivered from hopelessness and despair. Forgive me for resisting the Holy Spirit. Grant me a greater awareness of His presence. I choose to cooperate with You—to say no to ungodliness, to love my enemies, to show mercy, to forgive, to give generously. Clothe me with the power of Your Spirit; allow Jesus to be evident in all I am. Amen.

TITUS 2:11-12

For the grace of God that brings salvation has appeared to all men. It teaches us to say "No" to ungodliness and worldly passions, and to live self-controlled, upright and godly lives in this present age.

TODAY'S THOUGHTS ABOUT HOPE

Jesus gives us hope because He keeps us company,
has a vision and knows the way we should go.

Max Lucado

The earth's troubles fade in the light
of heaven's hope.

Billy Graham

We carry a bag of spending money in our hands,
but the bulk of our wealth is deposited
in the Bank of Hope.

C. H. Spurgeon

'Tis always morning somewhere.

Henry Wadsworth Longfellow

Faith is the Christian's foundation,
hope is his anchor, death is his harbor,
Christ is his pilot, and heaven is his country.

Jeremy Taylor

God is and all is well.

John Greenleaf Whittier

We must accept finite disappointment,
but we must never lose infinite hope.

Martin Luther King, Jr.

Great hopes make great men.

Thomas Fuller

Date:_____

Give Thanks: today I am thankful for . . .

_____

_____

_____

_____

_____

Worry Free: today I will lay aside all anxiety regarding . . .

_____

_____

_____

_____

Serving God: today I will serve the Lord through . . .

_____

_____

_____

_____

_____

_____

CHAPTER 18

TODAY, I WILL BE OPEN TO GOD'S TRUTH

PRAYER FOR THE DAY

Heavenly Father, thank You for sending us Your Word and Your messengers. Holy Spirit, help us to perceive our needs and Jesus' provision. May our hearts be receptive to God's truth. Send a spirit of repentance. Give us the boldness to follow and the willingness to proclaim Jesus as Lord and Christ. We offer ourselves today for Your purposes. Protect us, send us Your provision, and help us to recognize the season in which we live. May Jesus name be glorified, Amen.

PSALM 91:2

I will say of the LORD, "He is my refuge and my fortress, my God, in whom I trust."

TODAY'S THOUGHTS ABOUT GOD'S TRUTH

If we recognize God as the unique fountain of truth, we shall never despise the truth whenever it shall appear.

John Calvin

We know the truth, not only by reason, but by the heart.

Blaise Pascal

We must worship in truth. Worship is not just an emotional exercise but a response of the heart built on truth about God.

Erwin Lutzer

Peace is such a precious jewel that I would give anything for it but truth.

Matthew Henry

Where I found truth, there found I my God,
who is the truth itself.

St. Augustine

Not until we have become humble and teachable,
standing in awe of God's holiness and sovereignty,
distrusting our own thoughts, and willing
to have our minds turned upside down,
can divine wisdom become ours.

J. I. Packer

Peace if possible, but truth at any rate.

Martin Luther

No soul can be really at rest until it has given up
all dependence on everything else and has been
forced to depend on the Lord alone.
As long as our expectation is from other things,
nothing but disappointment awaits us.

Hannah Whitall Smith

Date:_____

Give Thanks: today I am thankful for . . .

_____

_____

_____

_____

_____

Worry Free: today I will lay aside all anxiety
regarding . . .

_____

_____

_____

_____

Serving God: today I will serve the Lord through . . .

_____

_____

_____

_____

_____

_____

CHAPTER 19

TODAY, I WILL CELEBRATE MY FREEDOM IN CHRIST

PRAYER FOR THE DAY

Lord Jesus Christ, I believe You are the Son of God and the only way to God. You died on the cross for my sins, and You rose again from the dead. I repent of all my sins and I forgive others as I would have God forgive me. I believe that You do accept me. Through Christ Jesus I am accepted; I am the object of Your special care. You really love me. Heaven is my home. I am a member of the family of God. Thank You! Today, I celebrate my freedom from any dark, evil spirit that took advantage of the pain in my life. Through the blood of Jesus I am free to live for the glory of my Lord. In Jesus name, amen.

ROMANS 8:1-2

Therefore, there is now no condemnation for those who are in Christ Jesus, because through Christ Jesus the law of the Spirit of life set me free from the law of sin and death.

TODAY'S THOUGHTS ABOUT CHRIST'S LOVE

As the love of a husband for his bride,
such is the love of Christ for His people.

C. H. Spurgeon

Christ did not die by accident.
He died voluntarily in our place.

Billy Graham

You don't have to be alone in your hurt.
Comfort is yours. Joy is an option. And, it's all been
made possible by your Savior. He went without
comfort so that you might have it.

Joni Eareckson Tada

Jesus departed from our sight that he might
return to our hearts. He departed,
and behold, he is here.

St. Augustine

Christianity is more than a doctrine.
It is Christ himself.

Thomas Merton

If you are a Christian, you are not a citizen of this
world trying to get to heaven; you are a citizen of
heaven making your way through this world.

Vance Havner

For the Christ-child who comes is the Master of all;
No palace too great, no cottage too small.

Phillips Brooks

What think we of Christ? Is He altogether glorious
in our eyes, and precious to our hearts?
May Christ be our joy, our confidence, our all.

Matthew Henry

Christ has turned all our sunsets into dawns.

St. Clement of Alexandria

Date:_____

Give Thanks: today I am thankful for . . .

_____

_____

_____

_____

_____

Worry Free: today I will lay aside all anxiety
regarding . . .

_____

_____

_____

_____

Serving God: today I will serve the Lord through . . .

_____

_____

_____

_____

_____

_____

CHAPTER 20

TODAY, I WILL SEEK GOD'S STRENGTH

PRAYER FOR THE DAY

Heavenly Father, we rejoice today that we are known by Almighty God. You are aware of our lives and interested in our well-being. Thank You for all You have done on our behalf. Grant us the strength to complete the course You have created for us. May the name of Jesus be lifted up through our lives. May Your truth be extended. May Your will be done on earth as it is in heaven. In Jesus name, amen.

DEUTERONOMY 33:25

The bolts of your gates will be iron and bronze, and your strength will equal your days.

TODAY'S THOUGHTS ABOUT SEEKING GOD'S STRENGTH

In sorrow and suffering, go straight to God
with confidence, and you will be strengthened,
enlightened, and instructed.

St. John of the Cross

God never gives strength for tomorrow, or for the
next hour, but only for the strain of the minute.

Oswald Chambers

God is in control. He may not take away
trials or make detours for us,
but He strengthens us through them.

Billy Graham

In my experience, God rarely makes our fear
disappear. Instead, he asks us to be
strong and take courage.

Bruce Wilkinson

We can be tired, weary and emotionally distraught,
but after spending time alone with God,
we find that He injects into our bodies energy,
power and strength.

Charles Stanley

It is not the cares of today, but the cares of
tomorrow, that weigh a man down. For the needs
of today we have corresponding strength given. It is
when tomorrow's burden is added to the burden of
today that the weight is more than we can bear.

George MacDonald

The weaker we feel, the harder we lean. And the
harder we lean, the stronger we grow spiritually.

J. I. Packer

We may live victoriously, not because we have any
power within ourselves, but because when we give
ourselves to God, He gives himself to us.

Norman Vincent Peale

Date:_____

Give Thanks: today I am thankful for . . .

_____

_____

_____

_____

_____

Worry Free: today I will lay aside all anxiety regarding . . .

_____

_____

_____

_____

Serving God: today I will serve the Lord through . . .

_____

_____

_____

_____

_____

_____

CHAPTER 21

TODAY, I WILL GIVE THANKS FOR GOD'S FAITHFULNESS

PRAYER FOR THE DAY

We rejoice today in Your faithfulness to Your people. Thank You for Your provision for our lives. We are grateful for Your kindness, mercy, and patience toward us. Forgive us for when we grumble and are ungrateful. You are a God of great love and watch over our lives. We pray especially today for the peace of Jerusalem. May Your angels stand guard over Your people. Let the enemies of Your people be confused and all their plans come to nothing. Our trust is in You, Almighty God, our Lord and our Redeemer. Amen.

PSALM 122:6-7

Pray for the peace of Jerusalem: May those who love you be secure. May there be peace within your walls and security within your citadels.

TODAY'S THOUGHTS ABOUT GOD'S FAITHFULNESS

God's work done in God's way will
never lack God's supplies.

Hudson Taylor

Knowing that God is faithful, it really helps me
to not be captivated by worry.

Josh McDowell

God is faithful even when his children are not.

Max Lucado

A God wise enough to create me and the world
I live in is wise enough to watch out for me.

Philip Yancey

In your relationship with God, He may let you make a wrong decision. Then the Spirit of God causes you to recognize that it is not God's will. He guides you back to the right path.

Henry Blackaby

God's mercy is boundless, free, and, through Jesus Christ our Lord, available to us in our present situation.

A. W. Tozer

God is able to do what we can't do.

Billy Graham

The knowledge that we are never alone calms the troubled sea of our lives and speaks peace to our souls.

A. W. Tozer

Date:_____

Give Thanks: today I am thankful for . . .

_____

_____

_____

_____

_____

Worry Free: today I will lay aside all anxiety
regarding . . .

_____

_____

_____

_____

Serving God: today I will serve the Lord through . . .

_____

_____

_____

_____

_____

_____

CHAPTER 22

TODAY, I WILL YIELD TO GOD'S PURPOSE

PRAYER FOR THE DAY

Heavenly Father, I rejoice in Your wisdom and strength. My ambition is to serve You with all my heart, mind, soul, and body. Holy Spirit, illumine my thoughts to reflect the glory of my God. I choose to yield myself to the purposes of Almighty God. May the Living Word of God come alive within me—to guide, direct, restore, and renew. Thank You for Your power expressed on my behalf. May the joy of my salvation strengthen me this day. In Jesus' name, amen.

PHILIPPIANS 2:3

Do nothing out of selfish ambition or vain conceit, but in humility consider others better than yourselves.

TODAY'S THOUGHTS ABOUT GOD'S PLAN

Either we are adrift in chaos or we are individuals,
created, loved, upheld and placed purposefully,
exactly where we are. Can you believe that?
Can you trust God for that?

Elisabeth Elliot

You weren't an accident. You weren't mass
produced. You aren't an assembly-line product.
You were deliberately planned, specifically gifted,
and lovingly positioned on the Earth
by the Master Craftsman.

Max Lucado

God has a purpose behind every problem.
He uses circumstances to develop our character.
In fact, he depends more on circumstances
to make us like Jesus than he depends on
our reading the Bible.

Rick Warren

God's heavenly plan doesn't always
make earthly sense.

Charles Swindoll

God's gifts put men's best dreams to shame.

Elizabeth Barrett Browning

Our heavenly Father never takes anything from
His children unless He means to give them
something better.

George Mueller

All God's plans have the mark of the cross on them,
and all His plans have death to self in them.

E. M. Bounds

It is the nature of God to make something out of
nothing. Therefore, when anyone is nothing,
God may yet make something of him.

Martin Luther

Date:_____

Give Thanks: today I am thankful for . . .

_____

_____

_____

_____

_____

Worry Free: today I will lay aside all anxiety regarding . . .

_____

_____

_____

_____

Serving God: today I will serve the Lord through . . .

_____

_____

_____

_____

_____

_____

CHAPTER 23

TODAY, I WILL SERVE GOD WITH GLADNESS AND JOY

PRAYER FOR THE DAY

Heavenly Father, awaken Your Church. May the Spirit of the Living God bring life to dry bones. Forgive us of indifference and idolatry. Open our eyes to the majesty and power of our Lord. May we serve the Lord with gladness and joy. May we turn away from the spirit of the world and embrace Your purposes. Embolden us to be powerful advocates for the kingdom of our Lord. Come quickly Lord Jesus, amen.

EPHESIANS 3:16

I pray that out of his glorious riches he may strengthen you with power through his Spirit in your inner being.

TODAY'S THOUGHTS ABOUT CHEERFULNESS

The practical effect of Christianity is happiness,
therefore let it be spread abroad everywhere!

C. H. Spurgeon

God cannot give us happiness and peace apart
from himself because it is not there.
There is no such thing.

C. S. Lewis

He is happiest, be he king or peasant,
who finds peace at home.

Goethe

Those who have been truly converted to Jesus
Christ know the meaning of abundant living.

Billy Graham

The most obvious lesson in Christ's teaching
is that there is no happiness in having or
getting anything, but only in giving.

Henry Drummond

Happy is the person who has learned the secret of
being content with whatever life brings him.

Billy Graham

There are many more flies caught with honey than
with vinegar and there are many more sinners
brought to Christ by happy Christians than
by doleful Christians.

C. H. Spurgeon

It is not fitting, when one is in God's service,
to have a gloomy face or a chilling look.

St. Francis of Assisi

Date:_____

Give Thanks: today I am thankful for . . .

_____
_____
_____
_____
_____

Worry Free: today I will lay aside all anxiety regarding . . .

_____
_____
_____
_____

Serving God: today I will serve the Lord through . . .

_____
_____
_____
_____
_____
_____

CHAPTER 24

TODAY, I WILL CELEBRATE GOD'S LOVE

PRAYER FOR THE DAY

Father, thank You for caring for me. Your concern and interest in my life are beyond understanding. I rejoice today that Almighty God has chosen me. My choice is to honor You. May the words of mouth and the meditation of my heart be pleasing to You. Help me to live in this age for the glory of my Lord, Jesus of Nazareth. May Your Word take root in my heart. Grant me a boldness to declare Jesus as Lord. May the power of Your Spirit direct my steps. I rejoice in my Lord and Redeemer, Amen.

LUKE 12:32

Do not be afraid, little flock, for your Father has been pleased to give you the kingdom.

TODAY'S THOUGHTS ABOUT GOD'S LOVE

God proved His love on the cross.
When Christ hung, and bled, and died it was
God saying to the world, "I love you."

Billy Graham

To be loved by God is the highest relationship,
the highest achievement,
and the highest position in life.

Henry Blackaby

God loves us too much to indulge our every whim.

Max Lucado

There is no limit to God. There is no limit
to His power. There is no limit to His love.
There is no limit to His mercy.

Billy Graham

Let us bring what is our own.
God will supply the rest.

St. John Chrysostom

Let nothing disturb you. Let nothing frighten you.
Everything passes away except God.
God alone is sufficient.

St. Teresa of Avila

Nothing can separate you from God's love,
absolutely nothing. God is enough for time,
God is enough for eternity. God is enough!

Hannah Whitall Smith

We should not be upset when unexpected and
upsetting things happen. God, in His wisdom,
means to make something of us which we have not
yet attained and is dealing with us accordingly.

J. I. Packer

Date:_____

Give Thanks: today I am thankful for . . .

_____

_____

_____

_____

_____

Worry Free: today I will lay aside all anxiety regarding . . .

_____

_____

_____

_____

Serving God: today I will serve the Lord through . . .

_____

_____

_____

_____

_____

_____

CHAPTER 25

TODAY, I WILL TRUST GOD'S PROMISES

PRAYER FOR THE DAY

Heavenly Father, thank You for the gift of Your Word. I rejoice in the great privilege of reading "The Truth." May each precept find the proper place in my heart. Holy Spirit, bring to life the reality of Almighty God within me—open my eyes to see and my heart to understand. The truth of Jesus Christ is my most treasured possession. I rejoice in the revelation You have brought to my life. In Jesus' name, amen.

PSALM 119:11-12

I have hidden your word in my heart that I might not sin against you. Praise be to you, O LORD; teach me your decrees.

TODAY'S THOUGHTS ABOUT GOD'S PROMISES

Our prospects are as bright as
the promises of God.

Adoniram Judson

From one end of the Bible to the other,
God assures us that He will never go back
on His promises.

Billy Graham

Let God's promises shine on your problems.

Corrie ten Boom

God's promises are sealed to us, but not dated.

Susanna Wesley

Don't let obstacles along the road to eternity
shake your confidence in God's promises.

David Jeremiah

God does not give us everything we want,
but He does fulfill His promises, leading us along
the best and straightest paths to Himself.

Dietrich Bonhoeffer

Faith is the assurance that the thing which God
has said in His word is true, and that God
will act according to what He has said.

George Mueller

Date:_____

Give Thanks: today I am thankful for . . .

_____

_____

_____

_____

_____

Worry Free: today I will lay aside all anxiety regarding . . .

_____

_____

_____

_____

Serving God: today I will serve the Lord through . . .

_____

_____

_____

_____

_____

_____

CHAPTER 26

TODAY, I WILL CELEBRATE GOD'S MIRACLES

PRAYER FOR THE DAY

Father, give us the courage to trust You for the impossible. Give us the boldness to step out and place our lives in Your care. Forgive us for our desperate attempts to remain at the controls. We need You to break into our lives with Your miraculous power. As we choose You, we expectantly look forward to Your interaction in our lives. We rejoice today in Your strength, concern, and watchfulness. In Jesus' name, amen.

JOSHUA 1:7

Be strong and very courageous. Be careful to obey all the law my servant Moses gave you; do not turn from it to the right or to the left, that you may be successful wherever you go.

G. Allen Jackson

TODAY'S THOUGHTS ABOUT MIRACLES

Faith expects from God what is
beyond all expectation.

Andrew Murray

God is able to do what we can't do.

Billy Graham

I never have any difficulty believing in miracles,
since I experienced the miracle of
a change in my own heart.

St. Augustine

Beware in your prayers, above everything else,
of limiting God, not only by unbelief, but
by fancying that you know what He can do.
Expect unexpected things.

Andrew Murray

I have found that there are three stages in
every great work of God: first, it is impossible,
then it is difficult, then it is done.

Hudson Taylor

It is wonderful what miracles God works in wills
that are utterly surrendered to Him.

Hannah Whitall Smith

God is able to do more than man
can understand.

Thomas à Kempis

When God is involved, anything can happen.
Be open. Stay that way.
God has a beautiful way of bringing
good vibrations out of broken chords.

Charles Swindoll

Date:_____

Give Thanks: today I am thankful for . . .

_____

_____

_____

_____

_____

Worry Free: today I will lay aside all anxiety regarding . . .

_____

_____

_____

_____

Serving God: today I will serve the Lord through . . .

_____

_____

_____

_____

_____

_____

CHAPTER 27

TODAY, I WILL TAKE REFUGE IN THE LORD

PRAYER FOR THE DAY

May the fear of God flourish in my heart and mind. May the purposes of Almighty God break into my awareness. May I be delivered from the bondage of selfishness and limits of my desires. Almighty God, I rejoice that You created me and are watching over me. You are my Redeemer, my Hope, and my Rock. Let new expressions of faith and courage arise within me. In Jesus' name, amen.

PSALM 34:7-8

The angel of the LORD encamps around those who fear him, and he delivers them. Taste and see that the LORD is good; blessed is the man who takes refuge in him.

TODAY'S THOUGHTS ABOUT GOD'S POWER

We may live victoriously, not because
we have any power within ourselves,
but because when we give ourselves to God,
He gives himself to us.

Norman Vincent Peale

God's work done in God's way will
never lack God's supplies.

Hudson Taylor

God works powerfully,
but for the most part gently and gradually.

John Newton

If you are strangers to prayer you are
strangers to power.

Billy Sunday

Our power is not so much in us as through us.

Harry Emerson Fosdick

In sorrow and suffering, go straight to God
with confidence, and you will be strengthened,
enlightened, and instructed.

St. John of the Cross

There is no limit to God. There is no limit
to His power. There is no limit to His love.
There is no limit to His mercy.

Billy Graham

Let nothing disturb you. Let nothing frighten you.
Everything passes away except God.
God alone is sufficient.

St. Teresa of Avila

Date:_____

Give Thanks: today I am thankful for . . .

_____

_____

_____

_____

_____

Worry Free: today I will lay aside all anxiety regarding . . .

_____

_____

_____

_____

Serving God: today I will serve the Lord through . . .

_____

_____

_____

_____

_____

_____

CHAPTER 28

TODAY, I WILL CHOOSE THE WAY OF TRUTH

PRAYER FOR THE DAY

Heavenly Father, may my life bear great fruit for Your kingdom. I need Your help. Holy Spirit, open my eyes to the invitations of God; grant me a willing spirit. Let courage arise within me, a new boldness on behalf of the kingdom of my Lord. May a longing for the things of God be unleashed within me as never before. Almighty God, may You go before me to prepare the path, may those who oppose Your purposes in my life be brought down. I rejoice in Your grace and loving compassion toward me. In Jesus' name, amen.

PSALM 119:30

I have chosen the way of truth; I have set my heart on your laws.

TODAY'S THOUGHTS ABOUT MY CHOICES

Men are free to decide their own moral choices,
but they are also under the necessity
to account to God for those choices.

A. W. Tozer

There are two masters, and you have to choose
which master you are going to serve.

Billy Graham

He who chooses the beginning of
the road chooses the place it leads to.
It is the means that determines the end.

Harry Emerson Fosdick

God always gives His very best to those
who leave the choice with Him.

Hudson Taylor

The choices of time are binding in eternity.

Jack MacArthur

God speaks to us through our conscience.
This may be a quiet voice that will not let us go
until we do what we know is right.
We must never silence that inner voice.

Billy Graham

Decisions become easier and simpler
where they are made not in the fear of men,
but only in the sight of God.

Dietrich Bonhoeffer

The discipline of daily devotion to God
undergirds decisions.

Edwin Louis Cole

Date:_____

Give Thanks: today I am thankful for . . .

_____

_____

_____

_____

_____

Worry Free: today I will lay aside all anxiety regarding . . .

_____

_____

_____

_____

Serving God: today I will serve the Lord through . . .

_____

_____

_____

_____

_____

_____

CHAPTER 29

TODAY, I WILL PUT GOD FIRST

PRAYER FOR THE DAY

Heavenly Father, I acknowledge You as my Lord and my Creator. Thank You for the gift of life and the privilege of serving You. Help me to discern Your pathways. May a love of Truth grow within me. Forgive me for my pride and my lack of cooperation. Today I choose a new beginning. I choose to give Your Word first place in my heart. I thank You for the extraordinary life You have created me for. May I have the courage and strength to choose You each day. In Jesus' name, amen.

PSALM 139:14

I praise you because I am fearfully and wonderfully made; your works are wonderful, I know that full well.

TODAY'S THOUGHTS ABOUT PUTTING GOD FIRST

There is an endless road, a hopeless maze,
for those who seek goods before they seek God.

St. Bernard of Clairvaux

A servant of God has but one Master.

George Mueller

To walk out of his will is to walk into nowhere.

C. S. Lewis

Live out your life in its full meaning;
it is God's life.

Josiah Royce

Let God put you on His potter's wheel
and whirl you as He likes.

Oswald Chambers

Don't pay much attention to who is for you and
who is against you. This is your major concern:
that God be with you in everything you do.

Thomas à Kempis

Christ is not valued at all unless
He is valued above all.

St. Augustine

Don't be a half-Christian.

Billy Graham

Date:_____

Give Thanks: today I am thankful for . . .

_____

_____

_____

_____

_____

Worry Free: today I will lay aside all anxiety
regarding . . .

_____

_____

_____

_____

Serving God: today I will serve the Lord through . . .

_____

_____

_____

_____

_____

_____

CHAPTER 30

TODAY, I WILL BEGIN A JOURNEY

PRAYER FOR THE DAY

Heavenly Father, today I choose to begin a journey, the pursuit of an extraordinary life. I want my life to bring honor to the name of Jesus. I recognize my frailty and my need for Your help. Holy Spirit, direct my steps. Forgive my sins. I forgive those who have brought pain to my life. I choose to turn my eyes toward the grace and power of my God and away from disappointment. I choose to accept God's invitations and to say no to selfish indulgence. This day, I determine to become an encourager of those pursuing God. Almighty God, through my life may Your kingdom come and Your will be done on earth. In Jesus' name, amen.

ISAIAH 1:17

Learn to do right! Seek justice, encourage the oppressed. Defend the cause of the fatherless, plead the case of the widow.

G. Allen Jackson

TODAY'S THOUGHTS ABOUT NEW BEGINNINGS

God specializes in giving people a fresh start.

Rick Warren

Beginning is half done.

Robert Schuller

Do noble things, not dream them all day long;
and so make life, death,
and that vast forever one grand, sweet song.

Charles Kingsley

One bold stroke, forgiveness obliterates
the past and permits us to enter
the land of new beginnings.

Billy Graham

The creation of a new heart, the renewing of
a right spirit is an omnipotent work of God.
Leave it to the Creator.

Henry Drummond

Start by doing what's necessary;
then do what's possible;
and suddenly you are doing the impossible.

St. Francis of Assisi

The wind of God is always blowing . . .
but you must hoist your sail.

François Fènelon

Are you in earnest? Seize this very minute.
What you can do, or dream you can, begin it.
Boldness has genius, power, and magic in it.

Goethe

Date:_____

Give Thanks: today I am thankful for . . .

_____

_____

_____

_____

_____

Worry Free: today I will lay aside all anxiety
regarding . . .

_____

_____

_____

_____

Serving God: today I will serve the Lord through . . .

_____

_____

_____

_____

_____

_____

CONCLUSION

Congratulations, thirty days of prayer is the beginning of an amazing journey. Once awakened to the reality of a living God, your life can never be the same again. A relationship with God is the most remarkable invitation ever extended to a human being. Allow prayers to continue in your heart and find expression in your words. God is listening.

ABOUT THE AUTHOR

Allen Jackson has served as senior pastor of World Outreach Church since 1988. Under his leadership, WOC has grown from a congregation of 150 to more than 10,000. Pastor Jackson has been a featured speaker numerous times at the Feast of Tabernacles in Jerusalem. His passion is to help people, wherever they may be, to become more fully devoted followers of Christ. His conviction in serving and effectuating a 24/7 church has touched people across the country and the world. Through Intend Ministries, Jackson coaches pastors across the nation and the world to greater effectiveness in their congregations.

Visit the News & Events Page for
WORLD OUTREACH CHURCH
wochurch.org/events

wochurch.org | (615) 896-4515 | 1921 New Salem Rd., Murfreesboro, TN 37128